LONDON'S WARTIME GAS B

A.G. Newman

Capital Transport

AUTHOR'S NOTE

This book was written following a talk given to the Friends of the London Transport Museum and also the London Historical Research Group of the Omnibus Society. It is a concentrated, London-centred version of a fuller work on the story of gas traction for road vehicles in the UK which I hope one day to complete.

I am indebted to a number of people for help in compiling this work. At the top of the list I thank my wife, Rita, for reading the drafts, improving my grammar and context, and persistently questioning points which were unclear in the earlier versions. I am also most grateful to the following individuals: Mr Laurie Akehurst, Mr Peter Bancroft, Mr Roy Bevin, Mr J. Graeme Bruce, Mr Brian Bunker, Mr Alan Cross, Mr Colin Curtis, Mrs Jo Holloway, Mr Fred Ivey, Mr Peter Jaques, Mr John Price, Mr J. David Smith, Mr John G. S. Smith, Mrs Rosemary Thacker and Mr Reg Westgate. I have avoided the use of footnotes, but a full list of sources is found at the end of the book.

TONY NEWMAN

ISBN 185414 194 5

Published by Capital Transport Publishing
38 Long Elmes, Harrow Weald, Middlesex

Printed by CS Graphics, Singapore

CONTENTS

INTRODUCTION

When the draft for this book was prepared in 1995, most people would have expressed surprise upon learning that buses can be persuaded to run on gas. This view would have changed during 1996 as experimental buses powered by compressed natural gas were given a public airing in Cambridge and Southampton, supported by British Gas. In Sweden there have been similar experiments with Volvo buses at Malmö which have led to plans for further trials in Great Britain. These recent moves have been directed at reducing pollution from vehicle exhaust gases in urban areas and have been given Government encouragement.

Around fifty years ago, given a free choice, gas was not the fuel that bus operators would have chosen, but in times of emergencies and shortages it is necessary to look around for alternatives to the conventional means of propulsion. As a matter of fact gas was employed in the propulsion of tramcars before the petrol engine was perfected – Blackpool St Annes and Lytham Tramways used a compressed gas system as far back as 1896. Since the United Kingdom has always been dependent on raw materials from abroad with which to make motor fuels, the advent of a world war causes serious disruption to those vital supplies. It does not seem surprising therefore that at such times of national emergency, operators should turn hopefully to any alternative source of power, and looking back into the history of road transport they rediscovered gas. In the period leading up to and during the Second World War, tentative experiments in vehicle conversion were encouraged at Government level and, as fuel deficiencies worsened, this encouragement was stepped up to coercion which resulted in a steady sprinkling of gas buses being seen on the streets of many towns and cities throughout Britain. This book attempts to record how London's buses were adapted in this way and how far they were successful in utilising gas in place of petrol. The main period of gas bus operation was short, lasting just over two years, but because of wartime conditions contemporary records are far from satisfactory for reconstructing a definitive history.

In the first place, extreme pressure of time resulted in much hasty, inaccurate and incomplete rendering of statistical returns so that the resulting records hardly registered the facts as they really were. Secondly the use of photographic film was very restricted and even in the fortunate event of securing some film, the possibility of the cameraman being taken into custody as a potential enemy agent was very strong especially if he pointed his camera at a street scene. Thirdly, the majority of unofficial recorders of these events were teenage boys: more mature and experienced recorders were either away in the armed forces or were heavily involved in their work and therefore had little time to travel around looking at buses. These dominant factors which applied throughout the war years determined the case that first hand knowledge of Producer Gas buses in the United Kingdom now rests with a small number of people.

Over the country as a whole, Leyland vehicles were most favoured for conversion, with AECs in second place, but in London, where there were few Leylands, the AEC double-deck ST type was the principal performer on producer gas; its short wheelbase and normally lively performance being well suited to this role. Despite the scarcity of information and some conflict between sources that have survived, the attempt has been made to place on record a sketch of this unusual form of transport and to recreate something of the atmosphere of the period.

CHAPTER I

THE FIRST WORLD WAR

It was not until 1917 that fuel shortages began to affect bus workings, by which time three years of war had placed increasingly severe restrictions on the use of petrol. The response of most operators was to cut services, but a few experimented with alternative fuels in order to maintain a reasonable level of services. First off the mark in meeting the challenge seems to have been Barton Bros in Nottinghamshire who had a Thornycroft bus running on containerised gas as early as the summer of 1916 between Beeston and Nottingham. During 1917 two Tilling-Stevens buses run by Bournemouth Corporation were converted to run on coal gas, and photographs appeared in Tramway and Railway World of a Daimler charabanc owned by S&J Wood of Blackpool, a Scottish Motor Traction single-decker, a Tilling-Stevens Petrol Electric at Falkirk and an unidentified Halley charabanc, all capable of operating on gas. In the same year Birmingham and Midland Motor Omnibus Company's vehicles were seen running on coal-gas in Worcestershire, Leamington, and other parts of the Midlands, while Chapman & Sons began an open coach service in June 1917 from Eastbourne to London (Victoria) twice a week using coal gas. Unfortunately the shortage of coal became more acute than the shortage of petrol and restrictions on the use of coal gas were soon tightened, thus limiting progress in this direction. Some operators carried out further experiments with running tramcars on gas, but this seems to have been done not so much in the interests of conserving fuel but rather as a means of making cost comparisons between various means of propulsion.

In 1917 the Gas Committee of Manchester Corporation calculated that 250 cubic feet of town gas costing about 10d would provide the equivalent propelling power of 1-gallon of petrol costing 3s 6d.

George Robbins and John Atkinson have recorded that in July 1918, the LGOC fitted B 533 with a balloon gas container which occupied the whole of the top deck. The container was filled with coal gas and the bus was run experimentally on one of the Hammersmith Road routes. One of the problems the authors describe was that as the balloon emptied, its silk envelope used to flap about uncontrollably. This phenomenon must have been extremely disconcerting to the many horses it would have passed!

Facing page top left
B 533 set up to operate on route 16, powered by compressed gas. The modification of the gas storage arrangements from an upper deck gas bag to gas cylinders beneath the seats is thought to have taken place in August 1918 and this photograph appeared in the transport press that month. However the lack of leaves on trees in the background gives rise to speculation as to the photograph's date.
Tramway & Railway World

Interior of **B 533**, showing location of gas cylinders beneath the seats. Four cylinders were fitted originally but later two cylinders of greater capacity were substituted.
Tramway & Railway World

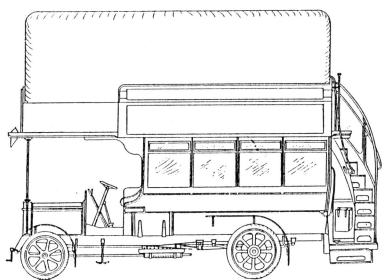

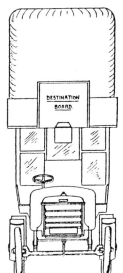

Drawings made in January 1918 of a B-type bus fitted with a gas bag for containing coal gas. It is believed that B 533 was fitted experimentally with this equipment and ran for a time on one of the Hammersmith Road routes in July 1918.

A further disadvantage was that the upper deck was no longer available to passengers and at the same time the overall height was increased, at least while the bag was inflated. It was not long before the gas bag was discarded and a short account of the failed experiment, together with pictures of the same bus as modified, subsequently appeared in *Tramway and Railway World* dated 15th August 1918. By this time it had been fitted with two compressed gas cylinders placed under the longitudinal seats, where initially four smaller cylinders had been placed. Each cylinder had a capacity of about 600 cu.ft of coal gas under 1,000 lb/sq.in compression. This was sufficient gas for a trip of only 20 miles, compared with 25 miles using the gas bags, but the seating capacity was thereby much increased. Externally the bus appeared little changed from the normal petrol driven version; however, the sharp-eyed observer might have detected the low pressure control valve and expansion chamber contained in a small box concealed behind the front destination board. All the electric lighting, both internal and external, had been replaced by gas lighting and some 300 lbs of electrical dynamo and battery equipment had been discarded as a result.

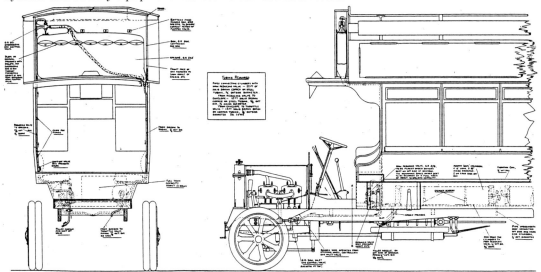

Left **Elevation drawings of a B-type bus equipped to run on compressed coal gas. Gas is stored in cylinders under the interior seats and released into a low pressure bag mounted behind the front destination board before being fed into the engine.**
Tramway & Railway World

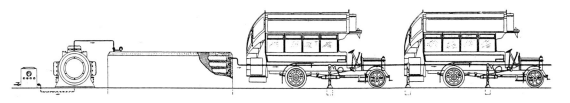

Drawings of B-type buses being recharged with compressed gas (to a pressure of 1,100-lbs per sq.in.) from a Reavell compressor. It was intended to install this equipment at Cricklewood garage. Tramway & Railway World

The bus was capable of running on gas or petrol and had a 12-gallon capacity petrol tank placed under the driver's seat for emergencies, and presumably for starting. The driver had no extra responsibilities when driving the bus as the supply of gas was regulated automatically in response to the throttle pedal. Although the trials of these experimental forms of propulsion for buses seem to have continued over several months, and despite the considerable involvement of the Metropolitan Police in these trials, the author has not been able to discover any files devoted to the subject at the Public Record Office. *The Electric Railway and Tramway Journal* carried a report in its issue of 19th July 1918 stating that the LGOC proposed to operate five buses from Cricklewood garage on route 16, all fuelled by cylinders of gas. It was intended to install a Reavell compressor at Cricklewood garage capable of re-charging several buses at a time from a 30,000 cu.ft storage unit, but no record has been found to show whether this was actually done. On 6th September 1918, the same journal reported that twenty LGOC buses had been licensed by the police to operate on gas compression. A Government Report published in 1919 also makes reference to this experiment and states that the twenty buses ran on route 16 (Cricklewood to Victoria). So far it has not been possible to discover the identity of these vehicles or the period of time when they were in operation. A contemporary official LGOC record of experimental vehicles includes a reference to B 4879 being fitted with gas cylinders in April 1919 but this does not make the situation any clearer.

Some interesting figures were quoted in *Tramway and Railway World* for 12th September 1918 relative to Scottish Motor Traction's experiments with flexible gas containers on their buses in Edinburgh. It cost about £50 to buy the container, but each container required continuous attention to keep it gas-tight and this was calculated to have cost the equivalent of 1.25 pence per mile. The gas itself was put at 2.17 pence per mile. When the cost of an attendant at the gas filling station was added in, the total costs were 3.5 pence per mile; considerably more than the cost of running on petrol at that time. The company took the view that this economy of materials for the war effort had outweighed the financial considerations.

CHAPTER 2

BETWEEN THE WARS

Between the wars a steady flow of experiments took place to find ways of harnessing alternative fuels for motor vehicles. In 1931 two Paris buses were successfully operated on compressed town gas over a lengthy trial lasting several months. (Town gas, i.e. coal gas, was often available from normal municipal supplies.) In 1933 Northern General put a gas bus into service in Newcastle with help from the Newcastle and Gateshead Gas Company. Later in the same year Birmingham Corporation ran a single-deck bus on town gas from the City Centre to Castle Bromwich for the British Industries Fair. In the next few years there were experiments in other towns such as Manchester, Wallasey and Burnley using town gas under high pressure in cylinders or low pressure in bags. Among a multiplicity of problems occurring in all these experiments, probably the most difficult to solve turned out to be that of recharging the vehicles, and in many instances further attempts were abandoned.

1933 also saw the first successful United Kingdom experiment with producer gas equipment on commercial vehicles. A demonstration of the new concept had first been given at the Paris Motor Show of 1931 as a prospective rival to compressed town gas. There had always been some fears expressed that town gas was highly dangerous stuff to carry around the streets, especially when compressed in cylinders. Producer gas systems had the merit that the gas did not need to be stored, as it was manufactured to meet the demands of the engine as the vehicle went along. A description of the way in which the gas was produced will be found on page 43.

In 1933 a company known as High Speed Gas (Gt Britain) Ltd developed the production of producer gas equipment, initially for goods vehicles and subsequently for buses. Later in 1933 this company bought up the Park Royal factory of the ailing Gilford Motor Company and formed a subsidiary company known as Gilford (HSG) Ltd. In 1937 they fitted to one of the last unsold Gilford chassis an AEC Regal engine with a gas-producer unit at the rear. It went on trials in Scotland in May of that year and was subsequently taken to London at the end of the month. Here it was presented for inspection by Members of Parliament outside the Palace of Westminster, after which it was fitted with a very basic bus body. It took up service in Scotland where it became No.76 (ST 9465) in the Highland

Transport fleet, and was put to numerous tests and trials including a spell in Glasgow in 1938. The results in Glasgow were not encouraging and the vehicle's poor acceleration came in for a lot of criticism. That year the HSG company amalgamated with Sentinel, and at the Commercial Motor Show were offering a Sentinel-HSG Producer Gas chassis in two versions; for 5-ton goods vehicles and 32-seater buses. An example of the latter was subsequently given a 14-day trial in Cardiff.

Coming closer now to the London Transport involvement, AEC had not been idle while the HSG work was going on. During 1937, probably realising that producer gas buses might become a necessity in the not too distant future, AEC had carried out a survey of what was on the market across Europe. They concluded that a French system – the Bellay system – which did not involve the use of trailers was the best so they formed a company, Gas Producers (Bellay) Ltd, to develop its principles in this country. It has not been possible to discover much about the Bellay business in France, but it is apparent that the equipment had the advantage of not requiring a separate trailer since it could be mounted directly on to the rear of a bus. This design, however, did not prove to offer the advantages that were promised. The Ministry of Transport was not willing to permit a general increase in the overall length of buses and so installation of the Bellay system necessitated either the loss of passenger seating – a result which was neither beneficial nor profitable – or a clumsy extension to the frame permitted under special dispensation.

High Speed Gas (Great Britain) Ltd's subsidiary company Gilford (H.S.G.) Ltd used a Gilford CF 176 chassis left over from the 1935 Commercial Motor Show and fitted a gas-producer unit at the rear. After trials in Scotland the chassis was demonstrated to Members of Parliament on 27th May 1937 and is seen leaving the Palace of Westminster.

CHAPTER 3

A NEW WAR, NEW TRIALS

In August 1939 the engineering staff at London Transport's Chiswick Works decided to carry out tests to compare the AEC-Bellay system with the trailer-mounted Government 'Emergency' Producer. As late as 26th September 1939 memos were still circulating at the Ministry of Transport to decide how to present regulations which would legalise the use of trailers on buses. Eventually it was possible to allocate five producer gas buses to Leatherhead garage and run them on part of route 406 (Kingston to Redhill).

ST 1100 carried the Bellay equipment mounted on a rear-frame extension and was initially road tested unladen on 24th September 1939. Several additional modifications were found to be necessary, including the provision of stronger springs to prevent the sub-frame fouling the ground when the rear wheels passed over pot-holes. After a further test between Tolworth Station and Epsom Grandstand ST 1100 was handed over to the Operating Department so that they could attempt to shadow an afternoon service bus on route 406 (duty LH 13) and devise an appropriate running schedule. On the morning of the day chosen the Operating Department were apparently eager to try their new machine and took it for a spin on the Great West Road where it experienced a total loss of power due to excessive condensation and only hastily improvised correctives served to get them back in time for the afternoon exercise. Five journeys were made over the section between Epsom and Kingston after which further gas temperature controls were added in order to reduce condensation. ST 1100 was put in the care of Leatherhead garage on 31st October 1939 and entered service briefly the following day, only to be withdrawn after a matter of hours at the request of the Mines Department which was concerned about 'undue publicity', though what exactly it meant by this is not clear. The bus was obliged to lurk in Chiswick Works out of the public gaze for a couple of weeks when it was deemed safe for it to venture forth. It returned to Leatherhead on 14th November 1939, entering service on the 406 route the following day.

Right **ST 1100 showing the AEC-Bellay gas producer mounted on an extension to the frame which required special dispensation from the Ministry of Transport. The equipment is encased in a wire gauze cage. The second picture shows the protective cage removed. The anthracite fuel hopper and fire-box are surrounded by gas filters and coolers. This equipment was used to carry out the comparative tests made in 1939–1940 but was discarded in favour of the trailer mounted producers.** Colin H. Curtis Collection

Meanwhile, ST 132 fitted with a trailer was road tested on 29th September 1939 and was intended to operate duty LH 12 from Leatherhead garage on route 406 from 1st November but, like its sister, was banished to Chiswick Works. While it was there improvements to the braking system, made necessary by the extra weight of the trailer, were carried out. The bus almost certainly resumed service on the 406 route on 15th November. These two pioneers were joined by ST 1119 which had only made its first run powered by gas on 11th November 1939. The section of route 406 between Epsom Downs and Kingston, over which they operated, included a moderate gradient known as Downs Hill. This caused late running of up to five minutes on journeys from Kingston and after a few weeks two of the gas buses were scheduled to run as service duplicates between Kingston and Epsom Town only, thus excluding the hill.

Two further changes to the gas bus schedules were made before and after the Christmas period of 1939 when heavy loadings of passengers led to fresh difficulties in time-keeping. Some replenishment of solid fuel was performed regularly at Kingston garage and time for this activity was included in the schedules.

In the new year the first trio were joined by ST 1105 and ST 1125, both with trailers, which began road tests on 7th February 1940. About this time there was participation by these gas buses on route 408 (Guildford to Warlingham) between Leatherhead and Epsom on their way to take up service on route 406. This was also when ST 132 was withdrawn for the fitting of a new engine, and reverted to petrol operation.

ST 1100 returned to normal working in mid-1940 but the remaining three ran, with some interruptions, until at least 3rd April 1941. In view of the poor hill-climbing abilities of producer gas buses it is assumed that they were always confined to the northern part of the route between Kingston and Epsom and did not venture on to Reigate Hill.

The anthracite used in these tests was marketed under the trade name 'Progasite' and manufactured by the Amalgamated Anthracite Collieries Ltd. A good deal of competition occurred between suppliers to secure the London Transport contract. Eventually government price control intervened and London Transport came to an arrangement with Cory's to collect the fuel from the nearest Great Western Railway station for 98/6d per ton with an allowance for the return of empty bags. This gave a running cost of 1.42d per mile on gas in 1940, compared with 3.0d on petrol, but for a true comparison the loss in efficiency and extra servicing costs need to be taken into account. It is believed that 'Progasite' continued to be supplied to London Transport well into the 1942-1944 period of gas bus operation.

Right **A GEP Trailer attached to ST 132 in November 1939. Note the warning notice to the unwary.**
London Transport Museum

Above **A trailer mounted Government Emergency Producer (GEP)** was subjected to bench tests as part of the 1939–1940 experiments. In this general view, the producer is located behind the measuring equipment and connected to a standard **ST-type** engine in the right foreground. The tests were carried out by London Transport in collaboration with the Fuel Research Establishment. Colin H. Curtis Collection

Above Right **A close-up view of the GEP** unit undergoing bench tests. The large fan is to simulate a 20mph air stream and the trailer wheels are regularly struck by rollers to reproduce the jolts and bumps caused by the road surface when the trailer is towed behind a bus. These tests were extremely painstaking and many modifications to the equipment were made after the results had been analysed. Colin H. Curtis Collection

There are still two more major threads to be woven into the background of this story. In 1938 the Tilling Group began some intensive work based on the French Gohin Poulenc gas-producer units. Their prototypes were tried out in the first six months of 1939 by three Tilling Bus companies; West Yorkshire Road Car carried out the first trials in March, followed by Hants & Dorset and Bristol Tramways in May. The manufacturing rights of the Gohin Poulenc process were acquired by Bristol Tramways and Carriage Company and the first 30 units were produced soon afterwards. During the course of further tests, the Chief Engineer of Eastern National devised an improved method of washing and filtering the gas before it was taken into the engine.

The other major thread to be traced concerns the British Government's input into the promotion of gas-producer units. In 1937 a Government Committee was set up under the chairmanship of Sir Harold Hartley to examine the prospect of converting motor vehicles to run on producer gas in the event of a national emergency. The Committee's Report was published in 1940 and envisaged a scheme for the manufacture of gas-producer units sufficient for the conversion of 10,000 road vehicles. Using British Patents, encouragement was given to the development – by the Fuel Research Station of the Department of Scientific and Industrial Research – of a unit which became known as the Government Emergency Producer (GEP). It had much in common with the Tilling design. However both these designs required the closest attention to filtration of the gas produced, otherwise marked wear on engine cylinders would occur. The chief ingredient in the problem of cylinder wear was the presence of sulphur carried over either as hydrogen sulphide or sulphur dioxide. Tests had shown that when coke was used as the solid fuel, cylinder wear could be as high as .001 of an inch per 1000 miles, whereas with anthracite this wear could be brought down to .0006 of an inch per 1000 miles travelled. One other unsatisfactory feature was that the existing rear-axle ratios of the majority of buses likely to be converted were a long way removed from the ideal for this type of power unit.

The response by the industry to these experiments was not enthusiastic. There were conflicting reports on the efficacy of rival units and the costs of conversion were substantial; each producer gas trailer cost around £90, which later rose to £106, and furthermore the availability of the most appropriate solid fuel for producer gas equipment was patchy. There were even some who argued that because a producer gas trailer ran on two wheels with rubber tyres, the extensive use of such trailers would greatly increase the demand for tyres and ultimately give rise to shortages in this commodity.

During the remainder of 1939 and in 1940, increasing numbers of gas-producer units (totalling between 40 and 50) were put into service with Tilling companies over the country. In contrast to this spread of producer gas operation, a number of municipalities converted a bus or two to compressed coal gas, or even in a few cases to low pressure coal gas with the ungainly gas bags on top. In 1941 the Tilling Group decided to intensify the work by designating two garages for operation with producer gas only. These were Maldon Depot of Eastern National with 9 buses and Cromer Depot of Eastern Counties with 12. On the other side of the country they had concentrated 7 producer gas buses at the Taunton Depot of Western National.

An unexpected supporter for producer gas conversions was the Earl Graham, Duke of Montrose. During his service in the Royal Navy he had taken command of a ship in 1907 which was propelled by producer gas. The experience had left a lasting impression on him and he was to be heard at regular intervals in 1941-2 speaking on this subject in the House of Lords and urging the Government to order the greater use of this alternative fuel. It subsequently transpired that he had an interest in one of the designs of gas-producer units which had not found favour with the Ministry of Transport. However, in the end the Ministry dug in its heels and presented the GEP as the only option open despite the uncertainty and unpredictability of future supplies of solid fuel. Presumably their thinking was based on the fact that the GEP was the only machine that could run happily on anthracite should the supply of coke become limited.

During 1941 there had been some faltering on the part of operators to maintain the numbers of gas fuelled vehicles, both passenger and commercial; they were finding them increasingly expensive and time consuming to maintain and more and more of the engineering staff were being called to the armed forces. There were some who questioned whether the saving in imported fuel would be sufficient to justify the use of large quantities of home-produced solid fuel to make the gas. Figures quoted in official reports about this time calculated that in the course of a year 10,000 producer gas vehicles would save only five sea-going tanker journeys from overseas, but would consume over 150,000 tons of solid fuel. However reports of increasing losses of tankers by enemy action caused less value to be placed on this comparison. A small number of MPs showed concern at this developing situation and questions were asked in the House of Commons on nine occasions between November 1941 and May 1942 about the use of producer gas equipment on road vehicles. The Ministry of Transport was therefore authorised to promote a scheme in April 1942 for the production of up to 10,000 GEP units. This was quickly followed, in May 1942, by a voluntary scheme whereby all bus operators with fleets of over 50 vehicles were encouraged to convert 10% to producer gas operation. This would involve the conversion of around 2,500 buses throughout the UK. A similar scheme for commercial vehicles was announced at the same time. Incentives to the operators consisted of advice and technical information being made available, but no financial assistance was being offered at this stage.

Left **A GEP** trailer detached from the vehicle, clearly showing the coupling arrangements for the tow bar, electrical supply and gas pipe. The parking legs at the front and rear are in use. This view is dated 15th November 1939.
London Transport Museum

Left **A GEP** trailer being inspected; perhaps by representatives from the **Ministry of War Transport** or **Members of Parliament**. The photograph is dated 'December 1940', but the fact that the London Transport driver is wearing a white cover on his cap and a summer dust coat suggests that the event took place before 1st October. The luxury of shiny hub caps was later abandoned for reasons of wartime economy.
London Transport Museum

By now the operation of producer gas vehicles had reached an all time low, as was admitted by the Minister of War Transport in response to a suggestion in the House of Commons that only 3,000 gas-producer units had been distributed since 1938 and that of these only about 100 were at present in regular use. Mr Noel Baker, the minister concerned, side-stepped the issue by saying that he was unable to confirm the figures but he thought well over 100 units were in use.

Unfortunately reliance on voluntary conversions did not bring the results hoped for and, against a background of acute shortages of many kinds, the Ministry issued a directive on 1st October 1942 that all PSV operators with fleets of 150 vehicles or more licensed at 1st May 1942 were required to convert 10% of their total fleet to producer gas operation by July 1943. However, it seems that very little attention had been given to the question of which companies were actually going to manufacture these units. A scheme had been operating since April 1940 to grant licences to manufacturers wishing to produce GEP units. Although over 40 companies appeared on the register, by January 1942 only three or four were active. Eventually it was agreed that Bristol Tramways & Carriage Company, which by this time had already become geared up to produce 560 units for the Tilling Group, should be allowed to produce 1,500 units slightly modified for general use. As a matter of detail, it may be of interest to London Transport vehicle specialists to know that the Bristol units produced for the Tilling Companies were given the classification 3T3, while the modified units were designated 3T4, thus echoing the class codes for buses in regular use by Chiswick works. The remaining 1,000 units would be produced by Wylie Harris & Co (which company had been formed out of High Speed Gas Transport Ltd). The trailer chassis was to be produced by J. Brockhouse & Co. At this stage it was agreed that the Ministry of Supply would be responsible for the manufacture of the units while the Ministry of War Transport would retain control over the specifications.

Even at this late stage there were attempts by some of the other manufacturers of gas-producer units to prove the superiority of their product. One who had been quietly working away in Swansea was South Wales Transport with their own 'Ravenhill' design developed in association with Amalgamated Anthracite Collieries. In August 1942 they challenged the Tilling Group to take part in a performance test over a 20-mile course. The Tilling Group had to admit that their Eastern National unit came out second best on this occasion, but it was by now too late for the Government to go back on their choice of the GEP and its close companion the Tilling unit.

By November 1942 the Ministry of Transport was not satisfied with the rate of conversions to date and a further directive was issued to many operators with fewer than 150 vehicles, requiring that they also convert 10% of their fleet.

Now we can look at how London Transport responded to the situation. It was decided to concentrate the first trials at Grays garage for three reasons: (1) the routes operated were self-contained and did not interwork with any other garage, (2) the site had vacant space suitable for a servicing area, (3) it was adjacent to Eastern National territory where there was already a great deal of experience in gas bus operation. Leatherhead garage was considered as a starting place because of the previous experience built up there but was not chosen since it had interworking with other garages.

While the experience of Eastern National staff was of use, the company had converted no double-deck buses and it was found in practice that the extra weight of a double-decker raised problems with braking. In an ideal world a more powerful gas-producer unit would have benefited a double-deck bus. London Transport initially had hopes of securing four types of producers for comparisons to be made. These were to have been the GEP, the Ravenhill, the British Coal Utilisation Research Association model (BCURA) and another government type known as the 21-Inch (the diameter of the hopper) but in the event there was no time to secure more than four Ravenhills and four 21-Inch Units as alternatives to the GEP.

The double-deck ST type was chosen for the majority of the conversions, although nine of the single-deck T type also received this treatment. These were all AEC petrol engined vehicles and the ST class had the added advantage of a short wheel base which was convenient when towing a trailer. The full conversion process involved increasing the cylinder bore by 10 millimetres and the compression ratio from 5 : 1 to 8 : 1. The increased compression ratio was a means of countering the loss of efficiency when a petrol engine was being fuelled by producer gas. Calculations showed that a ratio of 8 : 1 was about as much as the mechanics of the engine could withstand. The ignition timing was advanced to a very large degree and the carburettor (needed only when starting up) had its jets made smaller. In normal running it was the Gas Mixing Valve that performed the work formerly carried out by the carburettor.

A towing bracket was attached to the rear of the chassis and a gas hose was run from this bracket to the engine. From observations at the time it is evident that a process of partial conversion was applied to a proportion of the ST fleet at some stage after the initial batch of full conversions had been completed. Thus it was possible to see STs running in normal service with a towing bracket.

Whatever other work towards gas conversion had been carried out on such vehicles, it must be the case that they retained a petrol tank of sufficient capacity for a normal day's duty, and it does not seem clear what happened about the petrol tank upon complete conversion. The London Transport official manual for staff on Gas-Producer buses categorically states that the main petrol tank had been removed. If this is so one assumes that the tanks would have been steam cleaned and stored, but this would have taken up a lot of space somewhere.

Despite extensive enquiries, no clear information has come to hand. From evidence in technical reports it seems likely that the tanks remained in place to carry only very small amounts of petrol for starting up each day. One such report refers to the autovac body being filled to capacity with just one gallon of petrol. The autovac was a small pump unit located under the window of the front near-side bulkhead, normally used to raise petrol from the tank to the engine. It is known that at Grays garage it was intended to re-calibrate the petrol meters in pints instead of gallons and to reduce their pipes and nozzles to 3/8th inch diameters. It may even be that the normal petrol tank was simply disconnected in favour of a smaller new gravity tank and the manual was so worded to deter drivers from running on petrol after the initial start up.

The embryonic PSV Circle managed to collect a considerable amount of information about these partial conversions which it circulated to members through its early news-sheets. The term 'semi-gas' was applied to such buses in the news-sheets but such a distinction does not appear to have been made in the official records of London Transport. Immediately therefore there is an element of confusion thrown across the picture in trying to determine how many London buses were converted to run on producer gas. Of the sources available there are the official London Transport Allocation Books, which are printed records of the quantities of vehicles needed to operate every route and the garages at which these buses would be based; there are Traffic Circulars which are printed notices to inform staff of such things as changes to routes and stopping places; there are Schedules Books with staff timetables of all services.

The Chiswick Works records are unique; some of them were laboriously copied by staff and later found their way into private hands. Probably the originals of these works records do not survive. Finally there are records mainly compiled by boys, often bicycling round the country garages and scribbling their observations in note books and, but rarely, taking photographs. It is the last group which come closest to the truth, since most of the official printed records show what it was hoped to achieve and all kinds of contingencies in wartime could produce some very different results from those intended. In addition to these contemporary records, there have been useful articles in *Buses Illustrated* Nos. 35 and 38 and the Omnibus Society's booklet *London Buses in Wartime*.

Among the questions to which there does not appear to be a simple answer is, 'After the experimental gas STs of the 1940-1 period, which was the first standard producer gas ST with London Transport and when did it begin running ?'

At first sight, ST 171 might seem to claim that honour. Its photograph is in the London Transport Collection and it appears to be operating from Grays garage complete with a gas trailer and displaying running plates GY 4 plus a 351 route stencil. The original photograph is dated 5th February 1942, which suggests that it may be an artificially contrived official photograph – not an uncommon phenomenon so far as London Transport was concerned. This vehicle is not heard of again as a gas bus until late in the de-commissioning period, so that it may have been used for experimental work at Chiswick. An official London Transport report written in March 1943 stated, in relation to operations at Grays, that 'the first vehicle was running on the road at Whitsuntide 1942, and vehicles commenced in service a few weeks later'. In 1942 Whit Sunday was on 24th May.

There are three genuine contenders for the honour of being first: ST 335, ST 745, and ST 656. Chiswick sources record that ST 335, ST 656 and ST 745 were brought to the works for conversion on 2nd June 1942. The latter two were allocated to Grays on 19th June and relicensed there on 1st July. ST 335 stayed longer at Chiswick and joined the other two at Grays on 16th July when it was relicensed. Despite these three vehicles not being licensed officially until July, representatives of the staff of *Modern Transport* were treated by London Transport to a demonstration run in an ST gas bus at Grays which was reported on in their issue of 6th June 1942. The vehicle must have been well primed for the occasion as it was noted in the report that lighting up and starting occupied only two minutes. The same article reported that ST 656 performed well on a test run in the Ealing area on 2nd June by climbing Hanger Lane (a gradient of 1 in 8) in first gear with a simulated load of 48 passengers and 12 standees – a remarkably good performance which is suggestive of more special care to ensure success. Presumably at this time ST 656 was operating on trade plates, but the question posed in an earlier paragraph remains unanswered.

Six more STs arrived at Grays on 1st September (ST 401, ST 535, ST 594, ST 684, ST 720 and ST 791), followed by a further four on 1st October (ST 37, ST 63, ST 82 and ST 508), two more on 1st November (ST 262 and ST 462), when ST 335 was recalled to Chiswick, and four more on 1st December (ST 99, ST 118, ST 355 and ST 403).

On 22nd October T 273 was allocated to Grays as a gas bus and stayed there until 28th January 1943. When revenue service by these 20 gas buses which had reached Grays by 1st December actually began is not clear. The STs were all in Central Bus red livery, not the green of the Country Area where they were working. The Allocation Book dated 8th July 1942 foresees that 'from 30th September 1942 routes 370, 371, 372 and 375 will be gas bus operated'. Twenty gas STs were to be allocated to the 370/371/372 group on weekdays and fifteen on Sundays. The 375 was to be operated

by four gas Ts daily. Even that statement is not without its question marks! In the first place the numbers of buses allocated exceed the number we believe to have reached Grays by 30th September, and also at the time the Allocation Book was prepared a decision about withdrawal of Green Line services had not been fully resolved. In fact from 30th September route 370 became Romford to Purfleet, absorbing 372 (Grays to Purfleet), 371 became Grays to Rainham via Chandler's Corner (replacing Green Line 59), with a new 371A covering Grays to Rainham via Aveley (replacing Green Line 59A).

The 375 was the local Rainham service operated by T type single-deckers. There is just a possibility that at some time during July, August or September a gas bus operated route 372. Note also that no gas bus allocation is made for the Sunday-only route 351 (Grays to Oldchurch Hospital). This is all the more curious in view of the official London Transport photograph referred to above. Traffic Circulars appear to make no mention of these conversions going on in 1942.

Because of the LPTB practice of changing bus bodies on chassis, a system of class coding had been built up so that interchangeability could be recognised without recourse to stock records. For the guidance of engineering staff, it had become standard practice to fix small brass plates to each bus giving, among other details, the body or chassis class. These plates were placed on the dumb-irons of the chassis and usually by the nearside cab window on the body. Taken together, the codes 1ST for the chassis and ST1 for the body were read as 1ST1, which indicated the basic ST bus. Minor modification to either body or chassis was indicated by suffixes to read 1/1ST1/2, for instance. Major modification brought into use a new class code. With the advent of gas buses new chassis codes 4ST, 5ST and 6ST were applied to represent the standard STs, the ex London General Country STs, and the sole converted 'Bluebird' ST respectively. There is no evidence that conversion to gas resulted in any change to the body class code, nor is it known to what extent new brass plates were actually fitted to the converted chassis in the prevailing conditions.

Left **A close-up of the engine of ST 656 running on trade plates. The adaptations to producer gas are clearly to be seen. The photograph is dated 3rd June 1942.** London Transport Museum

CHAPTER 4

THE TRAILERS

The tests with the five STs at Leatherhead which began in 1939 led London Transport to the decision to use producers mounted on trailers. It had been found that mounting the equipment on an extension frame was expensive to install and complicated to maintain. The trailer on the other hand involved minimal work in converting the bus; servicing of the producer could be carried out away from the vehicle and, in the event of a breakdown, permitted a substitute producer to be connected with ease.

The costs of the producers have been variously quoted but, at the conclusion of the story when they were in store awaiting disposal, London Transport listed the original costs as follows: 18 inch GEP £120; Ravenhill £195; 21-inch £213 to £217. Standard trailers measured approximately 10 feet in length and 5 feet in width and weighed about 1450-lbs fully laden with fuel and water. Although there were some who alleged that a bus towing a trailer needed a relatively greater turning circle than a normal bus, this was not so and drivers were told in training to forget the trailer when turning. Trailers had to display a rear light and electrical connection was made to the bus by a domestic bayonet fitting. Unfortunately this was often forgotten when uncoupling took place; concentration being centred on avoiding the hot spots and stopping the trailer from running away since it had no brakes. They were fitted with retaining legs for parking purposes and failure to retract these on re-coupling sometimes led to further damage.

Once conversions began in earnest, the majority of trailers delivered to London Transport came from Bristol Tramways & Carriage Company's works. Here again there is conflicting evidence to be sifted. A file of correspondence between the Railway Executive Committee, London Transport and other interested parties survives at the Public Record Office. A schedule drawn up on 29th September 1942 records that by that time London Transport had taken delivery of 30 trailers; 20 of these were Tilling Units, 4 were 21-inch Units, 4 were Ravenhills and 2 were Bristol Units. Yet when London Transport got around to accounting for their stock of trailers they recorded only an initial 22 officially taken into stock on 29th December 1942.

Right **The GEP trailer attached to ST132, seen at Chiswick in November 1939 prior to entry into regular service. Note the polished hub cap.** London Transport Museum

It is evident that some had been in use from the beginning of that year when trials were resumed. Chiswick Works claimed two for the Experimental Shop and one for training while the remainder – however many that was – were at Grays who in turn had lent one to Epping for training purposes. During the next ten months a steady flow of trailers arrived from Bristol and were stored initially at three London Underground sites and latterly at Fulwell trolleybus depot. The Underground sites were at Wood Lane, Northfields, and Highgate, where the Underground staff found them something of a hindrance to the daily round.

Regular deliveries began on 1st February 1943, two months later than hoped, and then averaged seventeen trailers a week until a halt was called in mid-October 1943 by which time every available space had been used for storage. It fell to London Transport's Acting Chief Engineer to find accommodation for the trailers and by mid-April 1943 he was becoming desperate. He managed to negotiate an arrangement with the London & North Eastern Railway to store 250 trailers at the vacant premises known as The Old Forge, Stratford. These trailers were expected to be delivered by rail from Bristol.

Producer Gas Trailers   6042

(a) Fire Clinker.

To reduce the clinker now being formed, drivers are instructed to poke the fire at the end of each journey. Pokers will be located in the leg of the trailer.

(b) Log Sheets.

Staff are instructed that the gas producer trailer number as well as the bonnet number of the vehicle must be shown on all log sheets.

Producer Gas Trailers   6200

Fire Clinker.

To reduce clinker formation, drivers are reminded to poke the fire at the end of each journey.

Left **Extracts from Traffic Circulars issued in December 1942 and July 1943 respectively. Very often the task of giving the fire a few brisk jabs with the poker provided on the trailer was unofficially undertaken by an obliging conductor.**
London Transport Museum

Assuming the numbering system was reliable, a total of 634 trailers was received, the only non-Bristol trailers in the later deliveries being two from Neil & Spencer and two from Oxford & Cowley Iron Works. All were numbered in a simple series from 1 upwards; the Neil & Spencer trailers being numbered 235 and 236 while the Oxford & Cowley Iron Works ones assumed the numbers 237 and 634. The numbers were painted on the side of the frame, towards the rear and below the hopper. During 1944 several of the Bristol trailers were loaned to Neil & Spencer.

All the while that gas bus operation remained isolated at Grays the trailers remained fairly static, but once other routes became involved the trailers began to move around between garages and in and out of Chiswick Works. How these movements were carried out is not clear although it is worth noting that at least five vehicles in the Service Fleet of London Transport have been identified as being adapted in connection with producer gas work.

The first two were modified in July 1943. One was a Bedford WLB Box-van that had begun life as a bus with an independent operator. It bore the registration number AMF 595 and the Service Fleet number 149B. The other was a Leyland Cub tilt-lorry that always seemed to run on trade plates but had the Service Fleet number 183C. It is believed that 149B actually ran on gas for a time, but 183C was simply adapted to tow trailers rather than actually run on gas. The oldest was an ADC registered MY 3918 and carrying the Service Fleet number 3E. It was relicensed as a tipper lorry for gas servicing work in April 1944. Two Morris Commercial vehicles registered DGX 389 and EYK 399 bearing Service Fleet numbers 284M and 327M respectively were assigned to gas servicing duties in May 1944. It is probable there were others which escaped the records of both clerks and observers.

The official target which had been set for London Transport of 548 gas buses might well have required more than 634 trailers to include an allowance for overhauls, but the rate of conversion was falling so far short of the target that it was inevitable that a surplus of trailers would result. In fact records show that more than 200 trailers (probably 208) were never used. Twenty-two of the original batch were scrapped in April 1944 and a further 46 disposed of by May 1944. During September and October 1944, by which time the gas buses had reverted to petrol, many of the trailers were taken to the new Stockwell bus garage and stored there. Others languished forlorn and unused at the sites to which they had been delivered. They remained in London Transport care until a year later when, between August and October 1945, they were disposed of to the Ministry of Supply Surplus Stores Division at Great Missenden. Four trailers, numbered 259, 591, 597 and 603, appear to have escaped, either on loan or as a sale to Eastern National, and two others, numbers 171 and 194 spent some time at the Fuel Research Establishment at Greenwich.

CHAPTER 5

THE SERIOUS STUFF OF MAKING THE BEST OF IT

Having, so far as is possible, established the first batch at Grays we can take a look at what these gas buses were like to operate from the points of view of the maintenance staff, the driver and the conductor and what the passenger thought of them. As previously noted, the first garage chosen for gas bus operation was Grays and a number of the maintenance staff were taught about producer gas equipment by the Eastern National men. These skills were passed on but only a very small proportion of staff were really successful in mastering the new techniques. Mastery involved dealing with the very sensitive Gas Mixing Valve, alterations to the timing of the ignition, higher compression and specially shaped engine pistons. It was also essential to maintain a perfect seal along the tubes from the gas-producer to the engine. Sparking plugs needed constant cleaning, and all the pipes on the trailer had to be kept clean on a regular basis. Start-up at the beginning of each day was quite a delicate procedure. It began with getting the engine going on petrol, then lighting the fire with a coal-gas jet and gradually persuading the engine to give up its favourite food (petrol) and coaxing it to run on gas instead. Once the petrol was firmly turned off, the bus could be handed over to the public service driver.

The driver's task was probably overshadowed by a fear that the engine would stall, as, away from the resources and privacy of the garage, restarting was quite tricky. The driver had also to master the art of manipulating the Extra Air Lever at his left hand side; for at least the first half-hour of running each day this would require careful adjustment until just the right position was achieved for smooth operation of the vehicle. Gear changes would need to made at maximum revs in each gear and it would be necessary always to start from rest in first gear. A change of gear from top to third would be required at the slightest sign of a rising gradient although most routes chosen for gas bus operation needed to be free from hills. Drivers were instructed not to hang on to high gears because, if they did, suction through the fire would drop and by the time the lower gear was selected there would be insufficient gas available to take up the new gear. In addition a reversion to a crash gearbox, after the ease of the pre-selector gearboxes they had become accustomed to on the STL class, was an added burden for many drivers.

Right **ST 656 in June 1942 on a demonstration run being passed (very closely) by CXX 367 [STL 1657]. The GEP trailer unit is not representative of the final version used in London and the crew have omitted to ensure the registration plate is attached to the rear.** Imperial War Museum

33

Just a chance coincidence or one neatly staged ? A gas-bag private car passes **ST 656** as it waits while some more jumping on and off takes place on its demonstration run in June 1942.
Imperial War Museum

A certain amount of 'popping' was to be expected with this fuel; and there were undoubtedly times when 'popping' was far too mild a word for the sounds emerging! Reversing the bus with the trailer was bound to be difficult, but hopefully this could be avoided most of the while and some terminal points were re-located to overcome this potential hazard. On arrival at the terminal stand, if the lay-over time was 15 minutes or less, the bus had to be left with the engine revving quite fast, sometimes causing annoyance to local residents. Before setting off again it was recommended that the fire be given a few brisk jabs with the poker provided on the trailer.

The conductor's job was to keep an eye on the trailer from time to time and make sure it was not becoming red-hot, that the cooling tank was not boiling or that the tyres had not punctured. The conductor was also expected to make sure daydreaming passengers did not walk into the trailer after they alighted. A suggestion that a chain be placed around the perimeter of the trailer as a protective measure was not proceeded with, but some early photographs in 1939 (see page 29) reveal the presence of a steel fender bearing the words 'Beware Trailer' extending from each wheel to the towing bar. The smell of producer gas was not pleasant and some conductors with a keen sense of smell found it could become nauseating, especially when a following wind blew it onto the platform area.

The passengers on a gas bus were probably sensible to the smell which wafted around and also had a general impression that the engine had very little 'go' in it. The author's recollection is that apart from the high revs and the popping, once the bus was on a level stretch in top gear it was actually even quieter than a petrol bus, with a faint hissing noise sounding above the engine. A number of bus stops on slight gradients were moved to more level ground when gas bus operation began on a route. Schedules were very carefully revised to allow for the slower speeds of producer gas buses, even to the extent of giving greater time allowance on an adverse gradient in one direction of travel only. For example, the 301 route, southbound, was allowed extra time for the section from Aston Clinton up to the top of Tring Hill. A former driver at Tring garage recalled that they used to keep one petrol ST to run from Tring to Aylesbury and back to recover time lost by gas STs heading north on the 301 route. In the Epping area, the 396 route was allowed an extra minute in the southbound direction.

Usually arrangements were made to ensure that the routes chosen for conversion were such that buses passed the garage on each trip. This was especially important for the first few weeks as the mechanical staff were thereby able to come and look at the trailers at frequent intervals and satisfy themselves that all was well. It also gave the opportunity for refuelling to be carried out during the course of the day since the maximum range of a bus with a trailer full of fuel was about 80 miles. As trailers became more plentiful it was usually simpler to exchange trailers – or even bus and trailer –

at the garage than to attempt to refill a trailer with anthracite while it was attached to the bus. There were a few instances of lorries dedicated to carrying anthracite and refuelling buses at the terminus. It is presumed that these were drop-sided vehicles, but it has not been possible to identify them in the Service Vehicle fleet. The garages themselves had to be chosen for having sufficient space to store all trailers not in use plus, during the night, the buses with trailers. An open but secure yard was also necessary for stocking the anthracite and to give space for a lighting-up bay where the daily process of igniting the fuel in the hopper could take place. Space was further required for a pit into which ash, clinker and unburnt anthracite could be raked at the end of the day. Garages with facilities for diesel oil only would need to dispense with this type of fuel in order to handle the petrol necessary for starting gas buses. Grays garage became equipped to handle all three types of fuel for working their mixed STL and ST fleet, whereas Epping, due to its limited facilities, had to forgo its diesel STLs and was allocated central area STs in readiness for the gas operation. It is evident from all these necessary provisos that there was a complex series of choices to be made in arriving at a decision on the next route to be converted. Having established a firm pattern of operation of buses at Grays from October 1942, it was now felt that conversions could be carried out in other areas.

We left Grays at the end of October 1942 and now it is time to follow the progression of conversions on from there. In January 1943 six of the STs and the lone T were recalled from Grays and taken to Chiswick. The central area was selected for the next conversions, with Camberwell receiving gas STs in February 1943, ready to operate on the 36 route. This is the route most commonly associated with gas buses in people's minds because at the time it was probably the most photographed and it passed the main line stations at Paddington and Victoria. Servicemen and women on leave crossing London stood a chance of catching a tantalising glimpse of one of these unusual vehicles as they travelled between the two main line rail terminals. A question in the House of Commons, reported in Hansard on 4th February 1943, received a reply to the effect that (1) LPTB are at present operating 18 omnibuses on producer gas; (2) this number will increase to 550; (3) they require refuelling every 80 miles and that 27 service stations are planned for these operations. There is no indication of where the service stations would have been, nor indeed what constituted a service station apart from a bus garage. The figure of 18 buses at that date appears to match allocation records which show ten at Grays (ST 118, ST 262, ST 403, ST 462, ST 535, ST 594, ST 656, ST 720, ST 745 and ST 791), two at Camberwell for training (ST 37 and ST 684) and six at Chiswick (ST 63, ST 82, ST 99, ST 355, ST 401 and ST 508). In addition, ST 335, possibly ST 171, and T 273 were at Chiswick at this time but were probably in bits, undergoing experiments.

Right **Operating the specially constructed refuelling plant at Grays garage. The spent fuel has been emptied over a grille and the GEP hopper is about to be reloaded with a carefully regulated mixture of old (recycled) fuel and new fuel fed from two overhead conveyors. A load of 420-lbs of fuel per trailer was delivered in four minutes. This photograph was taken in October 1943.** London Transport Museum

Far right **The complexity of arranging turning points without reversal and at the same time not causing a nuisance is clearly demonstrated in these instructions from a Traffic Circular issued in October 1943.**

Producer Gas Vehicles— Turning Arrangements 6271

Damage is being caused to trailers on gas producer vehicles due to drivers reversing buses with trailers attached.

All turning arrangements have been approved to provide for turning without the need of a reverse and only under exceptional circumstances such as road obstructions should vehicles be reversed and then every possible care exercised in order to avoid damage.

Weybridge ("Ship").

IN OPERATION—MONDAY, OCTOBER 18TH, 1943.

(a) Vehicles from the direction of Addlestone with three minutes turning time only will turn as follows :— Set down passengers outside "The Ship" Hotel, circle island at junction of Monument Hill, Thames Street and High Street in an *anti-clockwise* direction and proceed to picking-up point at party wall of Nos. 43/45, High Street. Turning point only.

(b) Vehicles from the direction of Addlestone with stand time exceeding three minutes will continue to turn as follows :—

Petrol Bus : Proceed from High Street via Thames Street and Grotto Road into West Palace Gardens, reverse into Grotto Road and stand on the south side, west of junction with West Palace Gardens, by the electric sub-station box. Vehicles to face west and depart via Grotto Road and Thames Street to High Street.

Gas Bus : Proceed from High Street via Thames Street and Old Palace Road to stand in Grotto Road, south side, west of junction with West Palace Gardens by the electric sub-station box. Vehicles to face west and depart via Grotto Road and Thames Street to High Street.

London Transport was in correspondence with the Police in February 1943 about turning loops for gas buses on route 36 and proposed a loop on the north side of Peckham High Street, via Hill Street and Goldsmith Road, the stand to be situated in Bells Garden Road and the return via Frankton Road to Hill Street. Fortunately Brittains Service Station had ceased using one of their entrances which was in Bells Garden Road. At Hither Green the buses would leave Torridon Road at Hither Green Lane and proceed via Duncrievie Road to reach their normal stand at Springbank Road from the opposite direction. Both these terminal workings at Peckham and Hither Green officially received Police approval on 6th March 1943, three days after the gas buses began.

Initially, starting on 3rd March 1943, three gas buses were put to work each day on the 36 (West Kilburn to Hither Green) which were supplementary to the main service. There is photographic evidence that ST 174 was one of these and that ST 725 was another. The remaining initial allocation to Camberwell garage (ST 37, ST 63, ST 82, ST 262, ST 434, ST 588 and ST 684) took the total there to nine. Also during March several buses were placed for training or experimental purposes as follows: Leyton three (ST 277, ST 293 and ST 508), Croydon two (ST 689 and ST 764), Epping two (ST 95 and ST 521), Tring one (ST 429), Two Waters (Hemel Hempstead) one (ST 66), Addlestone two (ST 390 and ST 462), and Leatherhead one (ST 401). The following month the remaining STL duties at Grays were replaced by gas STs, officially from 21st April, bringing the total allocation to that garage up to 25.

It seems that it was intended to convert routes 301 (Watford Junction to Aylesbury) and 302 (Watford Heath to Hemel Hempstead) next, with Traffic Circulars giving a commencing date of Tuesday 1st June for gas bus operation – Tuesday being an unusual choice of day for the starting date of a new schedule.

The first licensed gas bus arrivals at Two Waters were ST 66 in March 1943 and ST 277 in April. They were followed by ST 352 and ST 1034 in April which were unlicensed. At the end of May a flurry of twelve unlicensed gas STs arrived (ST 2, ST 29, ST 43, ST 91, ST 259, ST 278, ST 326, ST 461, ST 473, ST 667, ST 684 and ST 751). A last minute arrival was ST 433, licensed on 1st June, presumably with the majority of earlier unlicensed arrivals, but official records are incomplete.

At Tring ST 390 and ST 462 were the first licensed gas buses to arrive and came in May from Addlestone where they had been since March. Earlier unlicensed arrivals had been three each in April (ST 360, ST 491 and ST534) and May (ST 90, ST 108 and ST 807). Two last-minute arrivals to complete the team on 1st June were ST 270 and ST 340. All unlicensed gas buses at Tring were licensed on 1st June.

ST 1034 at Two Waters is the only example of the 'Bluebird' class of STs being converted to gas.

Right **ST 535 apparently leaving Grays garage and going into service on route 371 in October 1943.** Someone has forgotten to check whether the trailer is carrying a registration plate; probably a frequent omission throughout the gas bus period.

Far right **ST 174 in Park Lane in service on route 36, clearly showing the final version of the GEP trailer unit, probably taken in March 1943.** John P Bennett Collection

Gas Producer Vehicles: Engines Idling 6133

It has been found necessary to alter the setting of the air valve which increases the idling speed of the engine when vehicles are stationary. Garage engineers have been instructed to apply the new setting and drivers are advised not to alter this or to be under the impression that anything is wrong because the engine speed when idling is higher than that of a normal type of petrol or oil bus.

Setting of Idling Controls 6168

Further to Item No. 6133, of Traffic Circular dated April 16th, 1943, it has been found advisable when the engine has to idle for a period of longer than five minutes, the speed of the engine should be increased considerably to maintain the fire in the hopper. In these circumstances, the extra air lever should be left in its normal open position and the hand throttle opened sufficient to ensure that the engine is running at a fast idling speed.

The temperamental nature of petrol engines being made to run on gas is indicated in these two extracts from Traffic Circulars issued in April and May 1943. Drivers were encouraged to ask Garage Engineers for demonstrations of correct idling speeds when stationary, but at the same time to remember that, under ordinary driving conditions, normal idling speed must be resumed otherwise gear changing would become difficult.

Facing page **A line up of GEP trailer units being prepared for service. A gas torch is being applied to the base of the fire box through a special aperture. This photograph is believed to have been taken at Grays garage on 22nd October 1943.** London Transport Museum

The possibility that all these conversions were re-licensed from the first of the month is another factor to consider in determining dates. Certainly the *Evening News* of 29th May 1943 foretold the start of gas buses on routes 301, 302, 461, 461A and 462 as from 1st June.

Meanwhile Epping, not mentioned in that *Evening News* announcement, had been building up a small fleet of gas buses during March and April and was officially converted with nine gas STs (ST 95, ST 236, ST 254, ST 262, ST 276, ST 356, ST 521, ST 669 and ST 671), covering an allocation of eight for routes 392 (Epping to Ongar) and 396 (Epping to Bishop's Stortford) starting on Wednesday 2nd June 1943, according to Traffic Circulars and another *Evening News* report. It is to be noted that six of these STs were relicensed on 1st May and possibly were used in service before the official starting date. Epping's other double-deck route, the 339 (Ongar to Warley) which was fed by the 392, was considered too remote from the garage for conversion to gas operation.

Also at this time routes 461 (Walton to Chertsey), 461A (Walton to Ottershaw) and 462 (Leatherhead to Staines) were converted to gas operation with seven STs allocated to Addlestone (ST 47, ST 192, ST 324, ST 335, ST 648, ST 730 and ST 801) for the 461, plus four Ts allocated to Leatherhead (T 273, T 352, T 354 and T 355) and five Ts allocated to Addlestone (T 288, T 347, T 350, T 353, and T 357) for the 462. A majority of the gas buses allocated to these two garages was relicensed on 1st June 1943.

Because the vehicles allocated for route 462 and all those based at Addlestone garage were likely to be used on services to Vickers Works at Weybridge where items vital to the war effort were being manufactured, most of these buses were hastily painted grey so as to make them less conspicuous from the air. The Allocation Books are again too misleading for any attempts to be made to use them for dating purposes. The Epping conversion appears in the revisions dated 5th May, whereas the 301/302 and the 462 do not appear until 6th October.

In May 1943 Hertford garage received gas ST 429 which was exchanged for ST 253 in June, and in July ST 37 arrived there but remained unlicensed. These were presumably for experimental or training purposes. The police urged London Transport at this time to maintain adequate supervision at all gas bus stands 'as it is most undesirable that children should have access to the gas-producer plant'. London Transport's reply in October 1943 was to the effect that they could not find enough staff to be able to comply with this recommendation. Gas bus trailers with their glowing fires and smelly gases must have been a great attraction for small boys!

In anticipation of the next stages of conversion, Willesden, Croydon and Catford received their first gas buses for training, while the numbers at Grays and Epping rose to 29 and 10 respectively by the end of 1943. There were 89 STs and 9 Ts operating on gas at the end of 1943 in the London Transport fleet. In addition there were London STs on loan to West Yorkshire Road Car based at Harrogate and running on gas between Harrogate and York, and others on loan to Coventry Corporation. Again, evidence as to numbers is conflicting. The PSV Circle ST Supplement records eight STs being loaned to West Yorkshire, but in a letter to *Buses Illustrated* published in issue number 51, a correspondent refers to the *five* London STs on loan *all* running on gas. The PSV Circle Fleet History on Coventry lists seven STs as running on gas in the city (ST 61, ST 153, ST 334, ST 385, ST 430, ST 806 and ST 926). The inclusion of ST 926 is the only example of a Tilling ST belonging to London Transport being so adapted, although there is evidence that a similar vehicle belonging to Brighton Hove & District was fitted with a gas-producer unit beneath the stairs, which suffered a mild explosion. The conversion of the London Transport Tilling ST is not mentioned in the PSV Circle's ST Supplement. The author of a later article on Coventry in *Buses Illustrated* issue number 114 confirms the number as seven and suggests that the open staircase of the Tilling ST resulted in passengers on both decks being subjected to the fumes.

By this time, that is the end of 1943, the last of the 634 trailers had been delivered to London Transport for working in the Greater London area. As noted in the previous chapter, this was far in excess of practical requirements and there were problems in finding space to accommodate them.

In December 1942 it was announced that for reasons of economy, a proportion of London's central area buses would appear repainted in a colour described as 'oxide red', which in practice turned out to be a brownish hue. The official records, however, did not list which actual vehicles changed colour in this way, but at least two gas STs (ST 270 and ST 521) were observed in this livery. During the second half of 1944 some of the red STs at Country Area garages were repainted in the green to which they were entitled; a process which had been foreshadowed in the press during February of that year.

The typical method by which the gas was produced may be described with reference to the diagrams overleaf. Solid fuel (preferably anthracite) is loaded from sacks into the top of the hopper which will take about 400lbs of fuel. After starting the bus engine on petrol in the conventional way, a lighted coal-gas torch is inserted into the bottom of the hopper to ignite the solid fuel. As soon as the fuel ignites, the torch is removed and air is drawn in through a vertical stack pipe to the water-cooled tuyere (or nozzle, where the gas torch was introduced) to produce a miniature blast furnace effect. The corrugated drum-like object which surrounds the hopper where the combustion is taking place acts as a water cooler for the tuyere, which has two effects: the water evaporates and the tuyere is blanketed by the steam which concentrates the core of the fire at the highest possible temperature, whilst at the same time the exterior is kept relatively cool. The gas that comes from the fire is a mixture of carbon monoxide, methane and hydrogen (which are combustible), a variety of impurities (most of which are non-combustible), and steam. This gas is then passed through three relatively large coolers followed by a water filter, a diluter and, finally, a water separator. These in turn reduce the temperature of the gas, remove solid particles, condense some of the water vapour and lastly remove the water itself. All these processes take place on the trailer and, as the name implies, gas is only produced when the engine of the bus demands it. Because of the tuyere's action any clinker is regularly formed in the same place at the base of the hopper and may be removed through a base plate, along with the ash. Waste particles and surplus water must also be removed on a regular basis through drainage valves. It was usually sufficient to empty these spent products at the end of each day.

In order to effect propulsion of the vehicle, the gas passes through an air-tight tube from the trailer, under the bus towards the engine, where it is mixed with air by three very carefully designed valve controls, known as 'butterflies' because they resemble butterflies' wings when open. Such valves are mounted within the tubes bringing the air and gas into the engine and open freely with an inward motion of gas but close against a flow in the opposite direction. The first of these valves is in the air passage and is controlled from the driver's cab by the Extra Air Lever. The other two, one located in the air passage and the other in the gas passage, are linked by levers and controlled by the throttle pedal.

In this way the mixture of air and gas is brought to the engine and is then ready for combustion in the engine cylinders in virtually the same way as petrol. The foregoing describes a process typical of the machines in use in London but numerous small refinements and modifications would have applied to each make of producer.

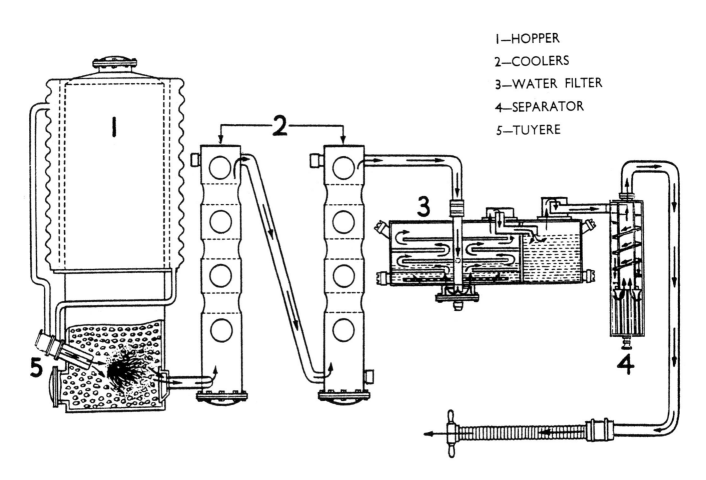

1—HOPPER
2—COOLERS
3—WATER FILTER
4—SEPARATOR
5—TUYERE

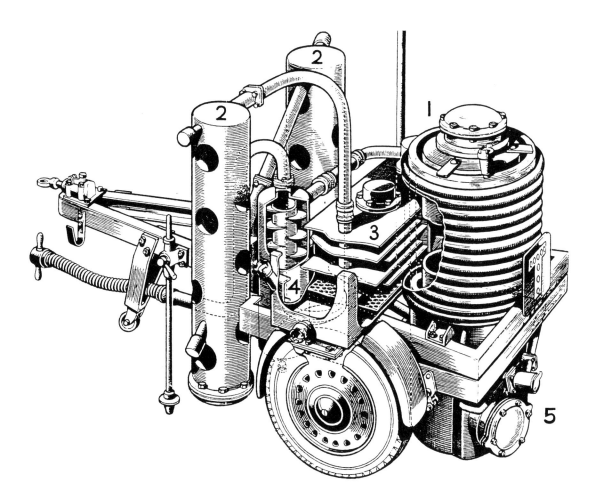

Simplified sketch of the later version of the GEP unit and (facing page) a diagram of how the gas is produced. London Transport Museum

GAS - PRODUCER BUSES

A Manual of Information for Maintenance Staff and Drivers

Foreword

These notes should not be regarded as a text-book. Indeed, knowledge of gas-producer equipment is increasing so fast that it would be impossible to produce a text-book that would not be out-of-date by the time it was printed. When you pass through your training you are given the best information that is then available, and the following notes do not pretend to do anything more than record some of those things which you should have to refresh your memory.

The best experience of this new form of working is that which you secure in the process of driving or maintenance. You may easily learn something which your instructors do not know, and if you acquire some knowledge of this kind, do not hesitate to advise your District Superintendent or your Garage Engineer.

You know that oil fuel in large quantities has to be used for the purpose of winning the war quickly, and gas-producer buses are being run not because we like them but because they do enable us to make a substantial contribution towards the great effort in which we are all engaged.

T. E. THOMAS
GENERAL MANAGER

February, 1944.

Left **Cover and Foreword of the Gas-Producer Buses Manual issued by London Transport.** Author's Collection

Right **Introduction and Appendix to the Manual,** the latter indicating the range of problems to which producer gas operation could give rise.

Introduction

London Transport has now commenced operating producer-gas driven vehicles, and this manual has been issued to give you a general working-knowledge of what the gas producer is, how it functions and the correct method of driving.

The producer being used by London Transport is of the trailer type, consumes home-produced anthracite fuel, and in a normal year will save approximately 6,000 gallons of petrol for each vehicle operated. In driving, a somewhat different method has to be adopted, and this is explained in detail later.

You may ask why convert an old-type petrol vehicle when the modern oil-engined vehicle is available. The conversion of a diesel engine is more complicated and costly than that of a petrol engine, and (what is more important) the saving in gallons of fuel is twice as much by converting a petrol engine. Ultimately, of course, it may be necessary to convert diesel-engined vehicles according to the availability of suitable vehicles for given routes, but at the moment the S.T. petrol-engined vehicles are being converted to gas operation.

Difficulties will no doubt be encountered at first in both operating and maintenance, but the Board is appreciative of this fact and feels that with your co-operation and goodwill the introduction of gas-producers will prove a success.

2

Faults : Their Indications, Causes and Remedies

INDICATION	CAUSE	REMEDY
Engine pulling badly and red-hot patch near tuyere	Clinker formation	Poke fire briskly
	Fuel too low	Stop engine and telephone garage for instructions
Engine pulling badly and red-hot section just below the tuyere	Air space in fuel underneath tuyere	Poke fire briskly and shake trailer to cause fuel to settle down
Engine pulling badly and hopper very hot around emptying door	Air leak	Stop engine and telephone garage for instructions
Engine pulling badly and will not idle	Air leak	See that emptying cock on separator is turned to OFF position. See that water level plug is fitted to water filter and screwed tightly home. Examine hopper, gas off-take pipe and coolers for fractures. Check securing nuts for tightness on hopper, coolers, gas off-take box, lighting box. Examine filling and emptying caps on filter and diluter tanks for tightness. See that petrol lever in driver's cabin is in the fully-closed position
Engine pulling badly	Coal jamming in hopper or fire may have died down, particularly after leaving stand	Poke fire briskly and shake trailer to cause fuel to settle down. Re-adjust extra air-lever, i.e. close it slightly until fire draws up again, then open to best running position whilst in THIRD SPEED
	Overheated hopper	Fully open extra air-lever whilst in THIRD SPEED, then slowly close it until best running position is found
Engine popping	Faulty ignition system. Insufficient gas	Slightly close extra air-valve and retard ignition, change into a lower gear for a short period
Tuyere tank boils excessively	Too little water in tuyere tank	Stop engine and telephone garage instructions
Irregular engine speed. Engine dies out when slowing down	Extra air-lever incorrectly set	Re-adjust lever to best running position whilst in THIRD SPEED

The continuing allocation of producer gas vehicles proceeded as follows: in the first week of January 1944 Croydon received its main consignment of gas STs, bringing the total there to 27, intended for use on route 197 (Norwood Junction to Caterham Valley). A month later Catford increased its total to 11 which were intended for use on route 36, and in April Camberwell received 18 more towards completing the conversion of route 36. Route 124 (Forest Hill to Eltham) out of Catford was the next route conversion, and during May that garage's stock of gas STs was increased to 31. Seemingly the next central garage on the list was to be Clay Hall and two gas STs were sent there for training purposes in May. Meanwhile the Allocation Book for 19th April 1944 showed route 36 calling for a maximum of 16 gas STs from Camberwell and 12 from Catford and also 12 gas STs from Catford for route 124 and 20 from Croydon for route 197. Thus the operation of gas buses in London had reached its peak by the end of June 1944 at which time it is possible to account for 149 STs and 9 Ts located at the garages mentioned, all fully equipped to run on producer gas on the above listed routes. In addition ST 196 was at Chiswick Works and ST 494 was at the Fuel Research Establishment Greenwich, thus making a total of 160 gas buses of which 11 were unlicensed. It is estimated that a further 130 STs were partially converted at this time and carried the distinctive towing bars.

It is extraordinarily difficult to assemble these statistics with confidence and unerring accuracy, although there seems little doubt about the 9 Ts. Even the official figures disagree and the Ministry of Transport table at 12th July (which must have been compiled with figures from London Transport) shows a total of 163 gas buses in the Metropolitan Traffic Area. This elusiveness of enough confirmatory detail may account for some of the omissions and conflicting information quoted in some previously published works on this subject. The article in *Buses Illustrated* No. 39 makes no reference to producer gas buses operating out of Catford garage, for instance; the other article in *Buses Illustrated* No. 35 shows discrepancies in the number of ST conversions, while the author of *London Buses in Wartime* appears unsure about the involvement of Catford garage on route 36. He suggests that Camberwell used gas buses on route 42 (Aldgate to Camberwell Green) while Croydon may have used them on route 59A. There is on record a remarkable first-hand account, from a lady who was a schoolgirl at the time, of a gas bus straying on to route 59B (Thornton Heath to Old Coulsdon) and not surprisingly failing to make it up Coulsdon Rise to Old Coulsdon, and there also exists a report from a reliable contemporary observer of a gas bus operating on route 1 (Lewisham to Willesden). Whatever the true number of gas buses operated by London Transport, there is a vast gap between the target of 548 set by the Ministry and the actual conversions achieved of well under 200.

CHAPTER 6

WHAT MIGHT HAVE BEEN

There is room for a good deal of speculation on which routes might have been converted, had the fuel supply situation worsened. There is evidence that Hertford Garage was next on the list for converting its 310/310A (Hertford to Enfield) routes in December 1943, but the easing of pressure on fuel supplies meant a relaxation in the need to use producer gas. The Country Area Allocation Book dated 8th July 1942 shows that, in addition to Hertford, the flatter routes operating from the following garages were being considered for gas operation: Crawley, Dorking, Hatfield, High Wycombe, Leatherhead, Northfleet, Reigate, St Albans, Watford (High Street) and Windsor. If Green Line services had continued after September 1942 (the temporary withdrawal was due to wartime economies), the following garages would have been included for gas coach operation: Amersham, East Grinstead, Guildford, Romford, and Staines. With fewer stops, gas operation of Green Line probably would have shown a lower fuel consumption per mile than bus routes.

There is evidence in official records that a Central Area single-decker, T 10, was fitted with a towing bar and appeared at Hornchurch garage in this state, but it is not clear whether it received the full modifications for producer gas operation.

In the Central Area, written evidence is to be found in a Police File at the Public Record Office for a number of routes being considered seriously for conversion in 1943. These include 27A (Highgate to Teddington) and 91 (Wandsworth Bridge to Cranford) which plans were eventually decided against because of difficulty in turning without reversing at Turnham Green Garage. The London Transport proposal for a turning loop round Turnham Green itself via Heathfield Terrace and Sutton Lane was not given police approval because of potential traffic dangers. The alternative police suggestion was for a loop via Clifton Road, Chiswick Common Road and Belmont Road. This proposal was not acceptable to London Transport, so there was a temporary deadlock. A compromise was however reached whereby route 27A would use the Belmont Road loop while the 91 would use the Turnham Green loop, but this plan was not proceeded with.

Gas operation of route 77A (Kings Cross to Raynes Park) would have involved minor re-routeing in Wimbledon, and turning via the Coach Station at Kings Cross. Consideration of this latter aspect of the route caused London Transport to arrange for air samples to be taken while a gas bus was under the covered area at the Coach Station. The analysis showed that there was a potential danger from the fumes which might adversely affect those people working in that confined area. (Memories of Omnibus Society London & Southern Counties Committee meetings being engulfed in diesel fumes in the post-war Kings Cross Coach Station offices make the gas bus fumes seem mild by comparison!) During the war, while coaches were off the road, the Kings Cross Coach Station at Crestfield Street was being used by buses terminating at Kings Cross in preference to standing on the busy highways in that area. The police were very much concerned about the proximity of the Coach Station to Argyle Square which they described as 'a place where children congregate to play and [where] standing buses will attract them and some danger may arise to those found tampering with the gas-producers'. The police therefore ruled that approval for gas buses to stand here would only be given if London Transport could provide an attendant at this point at all times when gas buses were standing in the area. Permission for the stand would also be withdrawn once producer buses ceased to operate. Again these factors weighed against the use of gas buses and therefore route 77A was not converted.

The next route to be considered for conversion, in July 1943, was route 6 (Hackney Wick to Kensal Green) which would have required a terminal variation at Kensal Green Station. This involved Chamberlayne Road, Station Terrace, Dagmar Gardens and Linden Avenue which had already been approved for ordinary buses on route 187 (Hampstead Heath to North Harrow) a month previously. However for a reason which seems to have been based on other factors, route 6 was not converted.

In a letter dated 28th August 1943 from London Transport to the Ministry of War Transport a proposal was made that the following routes be converted by the end of 1943:

1 (Willesden to Lewisham), 8 (Old Ford to Kingsbury), 15 (East Ham to Ladbroke Grove), 35 (Chingford Hatch to Clapham Common), 59A (Camden Town to Addiscombe) and 124 (Forest Hill to Eltham).

These conversions would involve Leyton garage for the first time and also would necessitate the allocation of additional gas buses at Croydon and Catford garages. The scheme required the placing of additional stands at Camden Town, Pound Lane at Willesden, Ladbroke Grove, Acton Vale, South Chingford, Streatham Greyhound and Forest Hill Station. Surprisingly, police approval was obtained for all of these applications, except the last which they considered too dangerous. This would have involved traversing Stanstead Road, making an acute right-hand turn into Rojack Road and returning to a stand in Stanstead Road via Rockbourne Road. However an unrecorded compromise must have been reached since it was only the 124 route which London Transport eventually decided to convert from the list of possibles outlined in the previous paragraph. Extracts from a London Transport report issued in March 1943 show that other garages considered for conversion but not proceeded with were Elmers End, Merton and Palmers Green. The Railway Executive Committee file, already referred to in Chapter 4, contains evidence that Upton Park, Victoria and two further unspecified garages were included for conversion in the plans made during the first half of 1943.

The next stage would almost certainly have brought in Willesden, Twickenham, Turnham Green, Battersea and Middle Row garages in March 1944 and Clay Hall in April 1944. The last conversion, that of at least a portion of buses on route 42 (Aldgate to Camberwell Green), is shown to have taken place by 23rd June 1944 when application is made for a revision of the Camberwell stand. This request may have given rise to fresh complaints in July and August by residents in the vicinity of Camberwell Garage who found the noise and smells very disturbing. A police officer visited the area and met with the LPTB Divisional Engineer who for some inexplicable reason is reported as stating the number of gas buses there as 'around seventy'. This was a gross exaggeration and must surely have arisen from a misunderstanding. Sadly the problem was soon solved when the houses in which the complainants lived were destroyed in an air raid.

There was also correspondence on the security risk caused by the glow from the fires of the producer units lighting up the sky in the Catford area, contrary to 'Blackout' regulations. During wartime it was an offence to show any light after sunset which might be seen by an aircraft overhead. An amusing misunderstanding occurred over this complaint when a London Transport official misread the wording of the letter and believed that an area of 30 sq. feet, had been illuminated, instead of 30 sq. inches! The incident had taken place at Perry Hill, Catford on 3rd March 1943 about 7.50pm. The offending vehicle was directed by an LPTB Inspector to 'the nearest terminus' and investigation showed that clinker had formed just below the tuyere, causing the exterior to become red-hot. According to the Drivers' Handbook this was Fault No.1 and could be remedied by a few jabs with the poker. The excessive glow referred to would only occur if gas-producer units overheated, and when the Ministry of War Transport Directorate of Vehicle Maintenance and Alternative Fuels was asked to comment on this possible hazard they admitted that overheating was certainly possible but that a foolproof remedy was not readily available. They made suggestions as to possible causes such as faulty maintenance, inefficient driving or incorrect fuel and they were willing to admit that although the fuel specification was well defined there were occasions when supplies of anthracite which were not up to standard inadvertently became available for use.

CHAPTER 7

IT'S ALL OVER BAR THE SHOUTING

Of the garages planned for gas operation, the Railway Executive Committee correspondence shows that by the time the scheme had ended, work was virtually completed at Catford, Clay Hall, Hertford, Leyton, Middle Row and Willesden, and preliminary work had been carried out at Battersea, Turnham Green and Twickenham, and possibly at Palmers Green and Watford High Street. Even though building work had not been started at Upton Park and Victoria there were items such as ventilators and lifting tackle specially purchased for these locations.

The last bus conversions to gas took place on 9th May 1944 when four STs were allocated to Camberwell (ST 21, ST 75, ST 571 and ST 761) and connected up to trailers.

From PSV Circle records we learn that one of the last incidents to affect the gas bus fleet, before regulations governing its use were relaxed, was the unfortunate loss of one member of that fleet (ST 637) which was damaged beyond repair by the flying bomb which landed at Elmers End garage in July 1944. The puzzle which arises over this statement is caused by the fact that official records appear not to include this vehicle as one which was fully converted for gas operation.

According to Chiswick Works records, a steady flow of reversions to petrol operation began on 16th August 1944, although there had been a few instances from the beginning of the month. The process continued to be recorded over the next four weeks until finally ST 594 at Grays was dealt with on 15th September and T 354 at Leatherhead reverted to petrol one week later. This evidence appears to indicate action well in advance of authorisation.

Traffic Circulars stated that routes 301, 392 and 396 would return to petrol operation on 30th August 1944. On 12th September the Ministry summoned a meeting of PSV Operators and announced that they might revert to the use of liquid fuel on all their vehicles. The gas-producer units would be left in the hands of the operators who were free to decide whether to continue with their use. However, one observer was at Grays three days earlier on 9th September and noted that gas bus operation there had ceased and one wonders on whose authority this action had been taken. The author of the article in *Buses Illustrated* issue number 39 states that all the Country garages ceased gas operation on 20th September, but that Grays continued for another two weeks. The conflicting evidence continues, even to the end! One of the police files at the Public Record Office contains a letter from London Transport dated 10th October 1944 which suggests that gas buses on route 36 had ceased. This file also contains a note of a telephone call from London Transport on 13th October informing the police that all gas buses had been taken off.

The small organisation at the Ministry of War Transport which had been set up under Viscount Ridley in May 1942, known as the Directorate of Gas Vehicles, was transferred to the Ministry of Fuel and Power in September 1944.

The Ministry's targets for conversion were left unfulfilled; in London the original target had been 10% of the licensed fleet of 5477 buses at 1st May 1942. This target was reduced to 4.6% by March 1944, but a figure of only 3% was achieved. The story was much the same around the country. The difficulty of keeping a good and adequate maintenance staff, poor performance of buses on all but the flattest routes, greater wear on moving parts of the engine, and the questionable saving of only 1d per mile on conversion to gas did not compensate for the capital costs and inconvenience attendant upon making the change.

The former gas buses, now freed from the burden of their trailers, continued to run with towing bars, but work to remove these began in earnest on 31st October 1944 and the last vestiges of gas operation were removed from ST 663 on 23rd January 1945.

Throughout the episode Lord Ashfield was conducting a lively correspondence with the Railway Executive Committee over financial aspects of the conversions. He took the view that the Grays building work came under the heading of 'Government Works to facilitate the working of wartime traffic'. The Ministry of War Transport could not agree, especially as they had already advised bus and coach operators elsewhere that they would be expected to bear all conversion costs themselves. It was not until 1945 that the finances were agreed on the following basis: all costs in respect of Grays would be entered as a special item of working in the Railway Control Account, as would the costs of subsequent bus conversions up to a total of £90,000; the building costs for service stations totalling around £165,000 would be regarded as coming under the 'Government Works to facilitate the working of wartime traffic' category. Presumably there had been a change of policy at the Ministry of Transport to accommodate this arrangement. Once the scheme was at an end it was agreed that London Transport should pay 50% of Costs for all items of equipment which they wished to retain.

The story of gas buses is almost at an end. Outside London, the Tilling companies chose to continue running some of their buses on producer gas to the end of 1944, including: Brighton Hove & District, Bristol Tramways, Eastern Counties, United Automobile and West Yorkshire. Two at Bristol survived until April 1945 but the record seems to be held by a non-Tilling company, East Midland Motor Services where the PSV Circle Fleet History records the last AEC Regal to be converted from producer gas to petrol in February 1946.

The service stations at Epping, Leatherhead and Leyton garages were demolished in 1946. Epping was one of the first to go in order to make space for the return of Green Line coaches. At Addlestone the service station was converted into a staff canteen about this time.

A rumour of gas buses operating on route 422 (Leatherhead to Boxhill Holiday Camp) from 2nd June 1948 and involving special turning points flits across the scene, but no reliable information about the vehicles or the duration of the experiment has come to hand. However, the involvement of Leatherhead lends credence to the rumour in view of the experiments in 1939 and at subsequent intervals, as will be shown in the next chapter.

Facing page
GEP trailer No. 24 after a fair stint in service, attached to **ST 480** at Grays garage. The trailer wheels no longer carry hub caps and it is surprising that the **ST** has not received protective netting on its windows.
Omnibus Society

Alterations to Services   6566

IN OPERATION—WEDNESDAY, AUGUST 30TH, 1944.

301. Watford—Aylesbury.

301C. Hemel Hempstead—Tring.

Revised timetable (5763). Withdrawal of gas producer vehicles, retimed for petrol. Route 301C extended from Berkhamsted to Tring over existing Route 301.

302. Watford Heath—Hemel Hempstead.

Revised timetable (5764). 15 minute '' peak '' service maintained a.m. weekdays.

307/A. Boxmoor—Harpenden.

Revised timetable (5771). Consequential to alteration to Route 301/2.

318/A. Bucks Hill/Sarratt/Watford—Two Waters/Chipperfield.

Revised timetable (5769). Consequential to alterations to Route 301.

377A, 377B. Apsley Mills—Markyate/Cupid Green.

Revised timetable (5768). Consequential to alterations to Route 301.

392. Epping—Ongar.

Revised timetable (5760). Withdrawal of gas producer vehicles and re-timed for petrol.

396. Epping—Bishops Stortford.

Revised timetable (5761). Withdrawal of gas producer vehicles and re-timed for petrol.

Traffic Circular notices in August 1944 in connection with the speeding up of journey times upon reversion of routes to petrol bus.

CHAPTER 8

COMEBACK

The final phase of the story brings us to 1952, when STL 2676 (one of the 'unfrozen' batch of STLs) was allocated for a series of experiments begun by the Ministry of Transport and concluded by the Ministry of Fuel and Power. Leatherhead Garage undertook to service the bus, and trade plates for it were issued to Neil & Spencer, the firm of engineers at Leatherhead. It was handed over on 24th December 1952 and appeared on the roads from time to time in 1953, painted grey and operating on producer gas fed from a trailer. On 28th December 1953 it could have been seen travelling along the coast road from Southampton to Eastbourne and back through East Grinstead and Reigate. Quite a sighting for spotters who happened to be around! There were hopes early in 1954 that it might be used in service but the chances of obtaining a Certificate of Fitness seemed slim. It did, however, shadow a service bus in June 1954 over route 411 from Reigate to West Croydon, with weights representing a full load of passengers, thus banishing the claim that producer gas buses could not climb hills. In November 1954 it was given its own 'ghost' timetable on route 406 (Redhill to Kingston) and ran Mondays to Fridays between 7am and 10pm under trade plates and driven by Dorking and Leatherhead drivers. The arrangement continued until August 1955, despite complaints in February 1955 by residents near Leatherhead Garage who, like the Camberwell residents in 1944, found the situation of waking each morning to the inevitable noise and smells quite unbearable. In August 1955, according to a file at the Public Record Office, the bus was taken to Hendon, though no subsequent information is given as to the reason for this or its fate there.

There is a passing reference to these tests in *Buses Illustrated* issue number 57 where it is suggested that the windows of this vehicle were painted over. The article also states that the Ministry of Fuel and Power had a Gas Research Station at Leatherhead, which probably explains why this curious arrangement was based there.

So far as is known, no further experiments with gas buses have been carried out in London but it now seems likely that some form of natural gas propulsion will form the basis for the continuation of this story in the next century. The recently announced fuel tax rebate which is available to operators of buses powered by compressed natural gas could prove to be the beginning of the next chapter of this fascinating history.

STL 2676, the subject of post-war experimental work on producer gas, in Leatherhead garage on 15th November 1953. The bus was of wartime origin, being one of a number built on a batch of chassis earmarked for other users but 'unfrozen' and supplied to London Transport in 1941.
Alan B Cross

APPENDIX: BUSES CONVERTED FOR GAS OPERATION

In the following list every ST and T for which any reference to gas operation has been found will be shown. The column headings require no further explanation, but the details shown under the heading 'NOTES' need clarification. The vehicles which are clearly known to have run on producer-gas in passenger service are shown in bold print and the principal garage or garages at which they were based is indicated by the London Transport Garage Codes as follow:

AC = Willesden - Limited or Doubtful Passenger Service
CL = Clay Hall - Limited or Doubtful Passenger Service
EP = Epping
GY = Grays
HG = Hertford - Limited or Doubtful Passenger Service
HH = Two Waters (Hemel Hempstead)
LH = Leatherhead
Q = Camberwell
T = Leyton - Limited or Doubtful Passenger Service
TB = Bromley - Limited or Doubtful Passenger Service
TC = Croydon
TG = Tring
TL = Catford
WY = Addlestone

CONVERTED BUT NOT USED indicates that there is evidence to show that these vehicles were converted to run on producer-gas but appear not to have run in passenger service or to have done so for a very short period only. Many of these will have been used for training and experimental purposes and some will have been working for much of the time on petrol with tow-bars but without trailers.

EQUIPPED BUT NOT CONVERTED indicates that evidence suggests these vehicles were fitted with tow-bars but at no time ran on producer-gas.

UNCERTAIN indicates that there is perhaps only a single reference to the vehicle being involved in the producer-gas scheme. This reference is probably due to an error somewhere in the evidence.

Column 1 = References to Gas STs in Fleet History LT7
Column 2 = References to Gas STs in Buses Illustrated No. 35
Column 3 = References to Gas STs in Extracts from LT Official Records
Column 4 = Contemporary Observations Actually Working on Gas
Column 5 = Actually Working on Gas at Coventry
Column 6 = In Harrogate W.Yorkshire, possibly working on Gas
Column 7 = Only record is in PSV Circle contemporary reports; being converted back from gas

	1	2	3	4	5	6	7	NOTES
ST	1	1	1					TC
	2		2					HH & TC BUT LITTLE USED
	9		9	9				GY
	14	14	14	14				CL
	15	15	15	15				Q
	16		16					CONVERTED BUT LITTLE USED
	18	18	18	18				TL
	20	20	20	20				TL
	21		21	21				Q
	23	23	23					TC
	25		25					EQUIPPED BUT NOT CONVERTED
	27		27					TC
	28	28	28					CONVERTED BUT LITTLE USED
	29	29	29	29				TL
	33		33	33				TC
	35	35	35	35				Q
	37	37	37					GY, HG LITTLE USED, Q & TC
	41	41	41	41				TL
	43		43	43				HH & TG
	45		45	45				TL
	46		46					GY
	47	47	47	47				WY
	48	48	48					CONVERTED BUT LITTLE USED
	56		56	56				Q
					61			
	63	63	63					GY
							65	UNCERTAIN
	66	66	66	66				HH
	67	67	67	67				Q
	68	68	68	68				Q
	69	69	69					GY
	75	75	75	75				Q
	76		76					TB, T & CL
	82	82	82	82				GY, Q & EP
	90	90	90	90				TG
	91		91	91				GY
	94	94	94	94				Q
	95	95	95					EP
	99	99	99	99				GY & TL
	102	102	102	102				Q

ST	1	2	3	4	5	6	7	NOTES
ST	108	108	108	108				TG
	109	109	109					TC
	118	118	118	118				GY
						120		UNCERTAIN
	130	130	130	130				Q
	132		132					LH
	133		133					CONVERTED BUT LITTLE USED
			141					UNCERTAIN
						146		UNCERTAIN
	151	151	151	151				CONVERTED BUT LITTLE USED
					153			
	155	155	155					TL
	158	158	158	158				Q
	160	160	160					GY
	165	165	165					GY
	166		166	166				Q
	167		167	167				Q, TL & GY
	171	171	171					UNCERTAIN
	173	173	173					CONVERTED BUT LITTLE USED
	174	174	174	174				Q
	176	176	176	176				TL, T & CL
	177	177	177	177				GY
					182			
	184		184					TB
	188	188	188					Q BUT LITTLE USED
	189		189					TC
	191	191	191					CONVERTED BUT LITTLE USED
	192	192	192	192				WY
	194	194	194					USED EXTENSIVELY AT CHISWICK
	196	196	196					CONVERTED BUT LITTLE USED
	199		199	199				Q & TL
	201	201	201					EQUIPPED BUT NOT CONVERTED
						202		UNCERTAIN
	206	206	206					CONVERTED BUT LITTLE USED
	207	207	207					CONVERTED BUT LITTLE USED
	213	213	213					TC
	216	216	216					CONVERTED BUT LITTLE USED
	218	218	218					TC
	221		221	221				TL
	225		225					TC & TL
	228		228					CONVERTED BUT LITTLE USED

ST	1	2	3	4	5	6	7	NOTES
ST	229	229	229					CONVERTED BUT LITTLE USED
	230	230	230					CONVERTED BUT LITTLE USED
	236	236	236	236				EP
	238		238	238				TL
	242	242	242					Q
	245	245	245					TL
	248	248	248	248				Q
					249			
	253		253	253				HG & GY
	254	254	254	254				EP
	258		258					CONVERTED BUT LITTLE USED
	259	259	259	259				WY, HH, TC & TL
	262	262	262	262				GY, Q & EP
	264		264					CONVERTED BUT LITTLE USED
	270	270	270	270				TG
	274	274	274					CONVERTED BUT LITTLE USED
	276	276	276	276				EP
	277	277	277	277				T & HH
	278	278	278	278				TC
			279					UNCERTAIN
	286	286	286					CONVERTED BUT LITTLE USED
	293	293	293	293				TC & TL
	299		299	299				CONVERTED BUT LITTLE USED
	303		303	303				Q
		308						PROBABLY ERROR FOR 303
					311			
	313		313	313				TL
	315	315	315					CONVERTED BUT LITTLE USED
	316	316	316					TC & TL
	324	324	324	324				WY
	326	326	326					TC
			328					UNCERTAIN
	329	329	329	329				Q
	330	330	330					CONVERTED BUT LITTLE USED
	331		331					CONVERTED BUT LITTLE USED
	333		333					EQUIPPED BUT NOT CONVERTED
					334			
	335	335	335	335				GY & WY
		337						UNCERTAIN
	338	338	338					CONVERTED BUT LITTLE USED

	1	2	3	4	5	6	7	NOTES
ST	340	340	340	340				TG
	341	341	341					CONVERTED BUT LITTLE USED
							344	UNCERTAIN
	345		345					GY
	346		346					CONVERTED BUT LITTLE USED
	349		349					CONVERTED BUT LITTLE USED
	352	352	352	352				HH & EP
	354		354	354				TL
	355	355	355					GY
	356	356	356	356				EP
	360		360	360				TG
			367					UNCERTAIN
	370	370	370					CONVERTED BUT LITTLE USED
	384	384	384	384				TL
					385			
	390	390	390	390				WY & TG
	392	392	392					CONVERTED BUT LITTLE USED
	393	393	393					CONVERTED BUT LITTLE USED
	394	394	394	394				Q
			396					UNCERTAIN
	401	401	401	401				GY, LH, Q, AC & TL
	402	402	402					CONVERTED BUT LITTLE USED
	403	403	403	403				GY & AC
	404	404	404					CONVERTED BUT LITTLE USED
						409		
	410		410	410				TC
	412	412	412	412				TL
	413		413					CONVERTED BUT LITTLE USED
	416	416	416					CONVERTED BUT LITTLE USED
	425		425					TL
	426	426	426					CONVERTED BUT LITTLE USED
			427					UNCERTAIN
	429	429	429	429				TG, HG & Q
					430			
	431		431					CONVERTED BUT LITTLE USED
	433	433	433	433				HH
	434	434	434					Q & GY
							436	UNCERTAIN
	443		443	443				Q
	444		444					CONVERTED BUT LITTLE USED
	445	445	445					CONVERTED BUT LITTLE USED

	1	2	3	4	5	6	7	NOTES
ST	446	446	446					CONVERTED BUT LITTLE USED
	452		452					CONVERTED BUT LITTLE USED
							455	UNCERTAIN
	456	456	456					CONVERTED BUT LITTLE USED
	461	461	461	461				EP
	462	462	462	462				GY WY & TG
	463		463	463				GY
	472		472	472				AC & TL
			473					UNCERTAIN
	477		477	477				Q
	478							ERROR FOR 479
			479					TC
	480	480	480	480				GY & TG
	483		483					TC
	485	485	485					CONVERTED BUT LITTLE USED
	489		489					CONVERSION NOT COMPLETED
	491	491	491	491				TG
	492		492					CONVERTED BUT LITTLE USED
		494	494	494				FUEL RESEARCH GREENWICH
	495	495	495	495				TL
	508	508	508	508				T & GY
	509	509	509					CONVERTED BUT LITTLE USED
			512					UNCERTAIN
	513	513	513					CONVERTED BUT LITTLE USED
	515	515	515					CONVERTED BUT LITTLE USED
	521	521	521	521				EP
	534	534	534	534				TG
	535	535	535					GY
							539	UNCERTAIN
	540	540	540	540				T & Q
	546		546					TC
	550		550					EQUIPPED BUT NOT CONVERTED
	551	551	551					CONVERTED BUT LITTLE USED
	555		555					CONVERTED BUT LITTLE USED
	557	557	557					CONVERTED BUT LITTLE USED
	558	558	558	558				TL
	560	560	560					CONVERTED BUT LITTLE USED
	561		561					CONVERTED BUT LITTLE USED
						565		
						566		

ST	1	2	3	4	5	6	7	NOTES
ST	571		571	571				Q
	573	573	573	573				TL
	578	578	578					CONVERTED BUT LITTLE USED
	588	588	588	588				Q
						592		
	594	594	594	594				GY
							597	UNCERTAIN
	598	598	598					CONVERTED BUT LITTLE USED
	606		606					CONVERTED BUT LITTLE USED
			607					UNCERTAIN
	608	608	608	608				Q
	609	609	609					CONVERTED BUT LITTLE USED
	618	618	618	618				GY & TG
	622	622	622					CONVERTED BUT LITTLE USED
	625	625	625					CONVERTED BUT LITTLE USED
			628					UNCERTAIN
	630		630					CONVERTED BUT LITTLE USED
			631					UNCERTAIN
	634	634	634	634				GY & EP
	637		637					CONVERTED DESTROYED BY ENEMY ACTION
	639	639	639	639				GY
	643	643	643					EQUIPPED BUT NOT CONVERTED
	645	645	645					CONVERTED BUT LITTLE USED
	646	646	646					EQUIPPED BUT NOT CONVERTED
							647	UNCERTAIN
	648	648	648	648				WY
	651		651	651				TC & TL
	656	656	656	656				GY
	661	661	661	661				TL
	662		662					CONVERTED BUT LITTLE USED
	663	663	663	663				Q & TL
	664	664	664	664				EQUIPPED BUT NOT CONVERTED
	667	667	667					HH & TC
	669	669	669	669				EP
	671	671	671					EP, Q & TC
	674	674	674					CONVERTED BUT LITTLE USED
							678	UNCERTAIN
							679	UNCERTAIN
	680		680					CONVERTED BUT LITTLE USED
	683	683	683					CONVERTED BUT LITTLE USED

ST	1	2	3	4	5	6	7	NOTES
ST	684	684	684	684				GY, HH & TC
	689	689	689					TC
	693		693					CONVERTED BUT LITTLE USED
	694		694					CONVERTED BUT LITTLE USED
	695	695	695					CONVERTED BUT LITTLE USED
	701	701	701	701				GY & TC
	710	710	710	710				TC
	713	713	713					CONVERTED BUT LITTLE USED
	714		714					TC
	717	717	717	717				TB & TL
	720	720	720					GY
	722		722	722				CONVERTED BUT LITTLE USED
	725	725	725	725				Q
	728		728	728				CONVERTED BUT LITTLE USED
	730	730	730					WY
	740	740	740					CONVERTED BUT LITTLE USED
	741	741	741					CONVERTED BUT LITTLE USED
	745	745	745	745				GY
						747		
	748	748	748					CL
	751	751	751	751				HH & TG
	752	752	752	752				Q
				754				UNCERTAIN
	756		756					CONVERTED BUT LITTLE USED
	761	761	761	761				Q
	764		764	764				GY
	765		765					CONVERTED BUT LITTLE USED
	776	776	776					CONVERTED BUT LITTLE USED
			780					UNCERTAIN
							784	UNCERTAIN
	791	791	791					GY & TC
	792	792	792	792				Q
							795	UNCERTAIN
	801	801	801	801				WY
	802	802	802	802				GY & EP
						806		
	807	807	807	807				TG
	808	808	808	808				GY
	814	814	814					T
	815	815	815					CONVERTED BUT LITTLE USED
		816						UNCERTAIN

	1	2	3	4	5	6	7	NOTES
ST	823		823					CONVERTED BUT LITTLE USED
	830	830	830					CONVERTED BUT LITTLE USED
	832	832	832					TL
					926			
	1034		1034	1034				HH
	1062		1062	1062				GY
	1067		1067	1067				GY
	1100		1100					LH
	1105		1105					LH
	1119		1119					LH
	1125		1125					LH

1	2	3	4	5	6	7	NOTES
		T 10					EQUIPPED BUT NOT CONVERTED
	T 273	T 273	T 273				GY & LH
	T 288	T 288	T 288				WY
	T 347	T 347					WY
	T 350	T 350	T 350				WY
	T 352	T 352	T 352				LH
	T 353	T 353	T 353				WY
	T 354	T 354	T 354				WY
	T 355	T 355	T 355				LH
	T 357	T 357	T 357				WY

SOURCES AND BIBLIOGRAPHY

Buses Illustrated No.35 'London's Gas Buses' Price, J.H. January 1958
Buses Illustrated No.39 'More About Gas Buses' Gillham, J.C. May 1958
Buses Illustrated No.51 Letters Column 'More on Gas Buses', Heard, M.H. May 1959

The PSV Circle/Omnibus Society Fleet History LT7 'The ST Class'

Commercial Motor 11th November 1938 'Sentinel-HSG Producer Gas Vehicles'

Modern Transport 6th June 1942

Tramway & Railway World 15th August 1918 'Compressed Gas Traction for Omnibuses'

'The London B-Type Motor Omnibus', Robbins, G.J. & Atkinson, J.B., Privately Published, 1970
'London Buses In Wartime', Price, J.H., The Omnibus Society c1968
'The STLs', Blacker, Ken, Capital Transport 1984
'Golden Age of Buses', Klapper, C.F. Routledge & Kegan Paul 1978
'Alternative Fuels for Public Service Vehicles', Troughton, H.J., The Municipal Passenger Transport Association 1940

Public Record Office Files: AN2 817, MEPO2 6786, MEPO2 7383, MT55 202, MT55 203, MT55 388, MT55 468, MT55 469, MT55 470, MT84 55, MT84 56 AND MT102 15.

H.M.S.O. 'Report on the Emergency Conversion of Motor Vehicles to Producer Gas' 1940